100 FAQ in Embedded Systems

Your Complete Guide to Crack Embedded Systems
Interviews

Author: Faayiz M

Edition: 1st Edition, 2025

Disclaimer

This book provides a collection of 100 commonly asked questions and answers in embedded systems. Each question is meant to serve as a starting point for understanding the topic.

While the answers provide a concise overview, many concepts require deeper study and hands-on experience to fully grasp. Readers are encouraged to:

● Refer to official documentation and technical books for in-depth knowledge.
● Experiment with real hardware and software to reinforce learning.
● Explore additional resources like research papers, courses, and open-source projects.

The content in this book is for educational purposes only. The author does not guarantee that the answers are exhaustive, as embedded systems is a vast and continuously evolving field.

Happy learning, and keep exploring embedded systems!

About the Author

Faayiz is an embedded systems engineer with extensive experience in firmware development, real-time operating systems (RTOS), embedded Linux, IoT and space tech solutions. With a deep passion for low-level programming, microcontrollers, and system optimization, he has worked on various industrial, space tech and IoT projects.

Beyond engineering, he is also a mentor, helping aspiring embedded engineers through technical discussions, brainstorming sessions and hands-on projects. His mission is to simplify complex embedded concepts, making them accessible and easy to understand for engineers at all levels.

Professional Experience

- Worked with real-time embedded systems, designing optimized firmware for STM32, ESP32, and ARM-based microcontrollers.
- Expertise in RTOS, low-power design, embedded networking (UART, SPI, CAN, MQTT) and TCP/IP protocols.
- Developed high-performance IoT and industrial automation solutions.

Connect with the Author

Email: faayizm98@gmail.com

"Embedded systems is not just about writing code—it's about building efficient, reliable, and innovative solutions that power the world around us."

Introduction

This book is a collection of the 100 most commonly asked questions in embedded systems interviews. Whether you are a beginner or an experienced engineer, these questions will help you prepare efficiently. Each answer is written concisely, with practical examples where necessary.

Who is this book for?

- Engineers preparing for embedded systems job interviews
- Students looking to build a strong foundation in embedded systems
- Professionals who want to revise key concepts

Basic Embedded Systems FAQ

1. What is an embedded system?

An embedded system is a specialized computing system designed to perform a dedicated function within a larger system. Unlike general-purpose computers, embedded systems are optimized for specific tasks.

Example:

- A washing machine has an embedded system that controls the washing cycles.
- A car's ECU (Engine Control Unit) is an embedded system that manages fuel injection and ignition.

Key Characteristics:

- Designed for specific tasks
- Real-time processing
- Resource-constrained (limited CPU, memory, power)
- Low power consumption

2. What are the key components of an embedded system?

An embedded system consists of:

1. Hardware Components:

- Microcontroller (MCU) / Microprocessor (MPU) – The brain of the system.
- Memory (RAM, ROM, Flash) – Stores program and data.
- Input/Output (I/O) Interfaces – Connects to sensors, actuators, displays.
- Power Supply – Provides necessary voltage.

2. Software Components:

- Firmware – Low-level code running on hardware.
- Operating System (RTOS/Linux) – Manages tasks and scheduling.
- Device Drivers – Interface between software and hardware.

3. What is the difference between a microprocessor and a microcontroller?

Feature	Microprocessor	Microcontroller
Definition	A general purpose CPU	A CPU with integrated memory and peripherals
Examples	Intel Core i7, AMD Ryzen	STM32, PIC, Atmega328

Used in	Laptops, PCs, Servers	IoT, Cars, Industrial Machines
Memory & I/O	External	Internal

4. What are the different types of memory in embedded systems?

Embedded systems use different memory types based on function and speed.

- RAM (Random Access Memory) – Temporary data storage (SRAM, DRAM).
- ROM (Read-Only Memory) – Stores firmware (EEPROM, Flash).
- Cache Memory – High-speed memory between CPU and RAM.
- Register Memory – Small, fast storage inside the CPU.

Example Usage:

- Microcontrollers use Flash ROM for program storage.
- Real-time applications need SRAM for faster access.

5. What is firmware, and how is it different from software?

Firmware is a type of software permanently stored in ROM or Flash memory of an embedded device. Unlike application software, firmware is closely tied to hardware and is updated less frequently.

Feature	Firmware	Software
Stored in	ROM	Flash Hard drive, Cloud
Examples	BIOS, Microcontroller Code	Windows, Android Apps
Updates	Infrequent	Frequent

Example:

- The firmware in a Wi-Fi router manages networking features.
- Android OS is software, while the bootloader is firmware.

6. What are real-time systems, and how are they different from general-purpose systems?

A real-time system guarantees that tasks execute within a strict deadline. They are commonly used in mission-critical applications where delays can cause failures.

Feature	RTOS	General-purpose OS
Timing	Time-sensitive	No strict deadlines
Example	Car airbag, satellites	Smartphones and laptops
OS	FreeRTOS, VxWorks	Linux, Windows

Types of Real-Time Systems:

1. Hard Real-Time – Missing a deadline leads to failure (e.g., Airbag).
2. Soft Real-Time – Missing a deadline affects performance (e.g., Video Streaming).

7. What is the role of a watchdog timer in embedded systems?

A watchdog timer (WDT) is a hardware timer used to detect and recover from system crashes. It resets the system if it detects software failure or hangs.

How It Works:

1. The watchdog timer starts counting.
2. The system must reset (kick) the watchdog periodically.
3. If the system fails to reset it (due to a crash), the watchdog forces a reset.

Example Usage:

- Automotive ECUs use watchdog timers to prevent car software crashes.
- Medical devices use watchdogs for continuous operation safety.

8. How does an embedded system boot up?

The boot process in an embedded system consists of:

1. Power-On Reset (POR) – System initializes.
2. Bootloader Execution – Loads firmware from ROM to RAM.
3. OS/Firmware Starts – RTOS/Linux initializes.
4. Application Runs – Device begins operation.

Example Boot Process (Microcontroller):

- Step 1: Microcontroller fetches bootloader from ROM.
- Step 2: Bootloader loads the main firmware.

- Step 3: System initializes I/O, peripherals, and interrupts.

9. What are interrupts, and how are they used in embedded systems?

An interrupt is a mechanism that allows a microcontroller to pause its current task and execute a higher-priority function immediately.

Types of Interrupts:

1. Hardware Interrupts – Triggered by external events (e.g., button press).
2. Software Interrupts – Triggered by program execution (e.g., system calls).

Example:

- A keyboard press triggers an interrupt in a microcontroller.
- A temperature sensor generates an interrupt if overheating occurs.

Steps in Interrupt Handling:

1. CPU detects the interrupt.
2. Saves current execution state.
3. Jumps to the Interrupt Service Routine (ISR).
4. ISR executes and returns to normal execution.

10. What is the importance of power management in embedded devices?

Power management in embedded systems is critical for battery life and efficiency.

Key Power Management Techniques:

1. Sleep Modes – Reduce power when idle (e.g., microcontroller low-power mode).
2. Dynamic Voltage Scaling (DVS) – Adjusts CPU voltage based on load.
3. Clock Gating – Disables unused peripherals to save power.

Example Usage:

- IoT sensors enter sleep mode to extend battery life.
- Smartphones reduce CPU frequency when idle.

Advanced Embedded Systems FAQ

11. What is memory-mapped I/O, and how does it differ from port-mapped I/O?

Memory-mapped I/O (MMIO) allows peripherals to be accessed as if they were memory addresses.
Port-mapped I/O (PMIO) uses dedicated I/O instructions to communicate with peripherals.

Feature	Memory-Mapped I/O	Port-Mapped I/O
Access Method	Uses regular memory read/write	Uses special I/O instructions
Addressing	Uses RAM Address space	Uses a separate I/O address space
Example	ARM cortex, RISC-V	X86 architecture

Example:

- ARM microcontrollers use memory-mapped I/O, so a peripheral (like UART) is accessed via memory addresses.

- Old x86 PCs use port-mapped I/O, where special IN/OUT instructions interact with peripherals.

12. What is the role of a Memory Protection Unit (MPU) in embedded systems?

An MPU (Memory Protection Unit) enhances security and stability by restricting memory access.

Key Benefits:

- Prevents unauthorized memory access (protection against buffer overflows).
- Enforces privileged vs. non-privileged mode in embedded RTOS.
- Improves reliability in safety-critical applications (automotive, medical).

Example:

- In ARM Cortex-M processors, the MPU prevents user-mode tasks from corrupting kernel memory.

13. How do cache mechanisms work in embedded processors?

Embedded processors use caches to store frequently accessed data and improve performance.

Cache Types:

1. Instruction Cache (I-Cache): Speeds up code execution.
2. Data Cache (D-Cache): Reduces memory access time for variables.

Cache Policies:

- Write-Through: Writes data to cache and memory simultaneously.
- Write-Back: Writes data to cache first, then updates memory later.

Example:

- ARM Cortex-A CPUs have L1 and L2 caches to improve execution speed.

14. What is the impact of Endianness in embedded systems?

Endianness defines how multi-byte data is stored in memory.

Type	Definition	Example(Hex 0x12345678)
Big-Endian	Most significant byte stored first	0x12 0x34 0x56 0x78
Little-Endian	Least significant byte stored first	0x78 0x56 0x34 0x12

Example:

- ARM Cortex-M (Microcontrollers) use Little-Endian.

- PowerPC and some DSPs use Big-Endian.

Why Does It Matters?

- Communication protocols must match endianness (e.g., network byte order is Big-Endian).

15. What is Direct Memory Access (DMA), and why is it used?

DMA allows peripherals to transfer data without CPU intervention, improving efficiency.

How DMA Works:

1. CPU sets up the DMA controller.
2. DMA transfers data between memory and peripherals.
3. CPU continues executing other tasks.

Example:

- SPI and UART use DMA to transfer large data without slowing down the CPU.

Benefits of DMA:

- Reduces CPU load
- Improves data transfer speed
- Allows real-time operation

16. How do you ensure real-time determinism in an embedded system?

Real-time systems require predictable execution times.

Techniques for Determinism:

- Use an RTOS with real-time scheduling (FreeRTOS, VxWorks).
- Minimize interrupt latency (disable nested interrupts).
- Use deterministic data structures (avoid dynamic memory allocation).
- Optimize task scheduling (avoid excessive task switching).

Example:

- Automotive ECUs require hard real-time behavior to control braking and acceleration.

17. What is the difference between polling and interrupts?

Feature	Polling	Interrupts
Definition	CPU checks status continuously	CPU responds only when needed
Efficiency	High CPU load	Low CPU load
Example	Checking sensor status in a loop	Button press triggering an interrupt service routine

Example:

- Polling is bad for power efficiency (e.g., checking UART buffer).
- Interrupts are better for event-driven systems (e.g., GPIO pin change).

18. What is priority inversion, and how do you solve it?

Priority Inversion happens when a high-priority task is blocked by a low-priority task.

Example Scenario:

- A low-priority task holds a mutex.
- A high-priority task needs the same mutex but is blocked.

Solutions:

1. Priority Inheritance: Temporarily boosts low-priority task priority.
2. Priority Ceiling: Pre-assigns a fixed priority to avoid conflicts.

Example Usage:

- Mars Pathfinder rover had a priority inversion bug, causing system resets.

19. How does watchdog timer configuration affect system reliability?

A watchdog timer (WDT) resets the system if the software fails.

Best Practices for Watchdog Timers:

- Choose appropriate timeout values (too short causes unnecessary resets).
- Reset watchdog carefully (avoid clearing it in infinite loops).
- Use windowed watchdogs to prevent premature resets.

Example Usage:

- Medical devices use watchdog timers to ensure continuous operation.

20. What are the key challenges in designing low-power embedded systems?

Common Challenges:

1. Balancing power and performance (high-speed CPUs consume more power).
2. Minimizing leakage currents in sleep modes.
3. Choosing the right battery technology (Li-ion vs. NiMH).
4. Efficient power conversion (DC-DC converters reduce power loss).

Solutions:

- Use low-power MCUs (e.g., STM32L series).

- Optimize sleep and idle states.
- Implement dynamic voltage scaling.

Example Usage:

- IoT devices use aggressive power management to extend battery life.

Basic Microcontroller & Firmware FAQ

This section covers fundamental microcontroller concepts for beginners, followed by advanced microcontroller and firmware topics for experienced engineers.

1. What is a microcontroller, and how does it work?

A microcontroller (MCU) is a small, self-contained computing system that includes a CPU, memory, and I/O peripherals on a single chip. It is used for controlling specific embedded applications.

Key Features:

- Integrated RAM, ROM, I/O ports, and timers
- Works with low power consumption
- Used in IoT devices, consumer electronics, automotive systems

Example:

An Arduino (ATmega328P) microcontroller reads a sensor and turns on an LED when a threshold is crossed.

2. How does a microcontroller differ from a SoC?

Feature	Microcontroller (MCU)	System on Chip (SoC)
Definition	A compact IC with CPU, RAM, Flash, and peripherals for embedded applications.	A highly integrated IC with CPU, GPU, RAM, storage, and connectivity.
Complexity	Designed for simple, dedicated tasks.	More complex and capable of handling advanced computing.
Processing Power	Uses low-power processors (e.g., ARM Cortex-M, 8-bit AVR).	Uses high-performance processors (e.g., ARM Cortex-A, Apple M-series).

Memory & Storage	Built-in Flash and SRAM (few KBs to MBs).	Uses external RAM (DDR) and storage (eMMC, NVMe).
Operating System	Runs bare-metal code or RTOS (FreeRTOS, Zephyr).	Runs full OS like Linux, Android, or Windows.
Applications	IoT devices, industrial automation, home appliances, automotive ECUs.	Smartphones, Raspberry Pi, AI applications, gaming consoles.

3. What are GPIOs, and why are they important?

General-Purpose Input/Output (GPIO) pins allow a microcontroller to interface with external devices like sensors, motors, and LEDs.

GPIO Modes:

- Input Mode – Reads sensor data.
- Output Mode – Controls external devices.
- Alternate Function Mode – Used for communication (SPI, UART, I2C).

Example:

Pressing a button (input) to turn on an LED (output).

4. What are the different types of timers in microcontrollers?

Microcontrollers use timers to generate precise time delays, measure signals, and control tasks.

Timer Type	Function
Counter Timer	Counts external pulses
PWM timer	Controls motor speed
Watchdog timer or WDT	Resets MCU if software fails or got hung

Example:

A PWM timer adjusts a DC motor's speed in an embedded system.

5. What is an interrupt, and how does it work?

An interrupt allows a microcontroller to respond to external or internal events immediately, without polling.

Types of Interrupts:

- Hardware Interrupt – Triggered by external events (e.g., button press).
- Software Interrupt – Triggered by a program (e.g., system call).

Example:

When a temperature sensor detects overheating, an interrupt triggers an emergency shutdown.

6. What is a bootloader, and why is it used?

A bootloader is a small firmware program that allows a microcontroller to load and update the main firmware.

Functions of a Bootloader:

- Initializes hardware at startup.
- Loads firmware from Flash to RAM.
- Allows over-the-air (OTA) firmware updates.

Example:

ESP8266 Wi-Fi module uses a bootloader to update firmware via Wi-Fi.

7. What is Flash memory, and how does it differ from RAM?

Feature	Flash Memory	RAM
Purpose	Stores firmware permanently	Temporary working memory

volatility	Non-volatile(retains data after power-off)	Volatile(loses data when powered off)
Example	Stores microcontrollers firmware	Stores variables and stack

Example:

A microcontroller's Flash memory holds the program, while RAM stores sensor data during execution.

8. What is UART, and how does it work?

UART (Universal Asynchronous Receiver-Transmitter) is a serial communication protocol used for device-to-device communication.

UART Communication:

- Transmits data byte-by-byte over TX and RX lines.
- Uses start and stop bits instead of a clock.

Example:

- Arduino communicates with a PC over UART (via USB).
- GPS modules send data to microcontrollers over UART.

9. How to configure WDT?

- Enable the Watchdog Timer – Configure the WDT with a timeout period.
- Feed the Watchdog – Reset the WDT timer periodically in the main loop or a specific task.
- Allow Auto-Reset – If the firmware crashes or fails to reset the WDT, the system restarts.

10. What are registers why it is required?

- Registers are small, high-speed memory units inside a microcontroller or CPU that store temporary data, instructions, and control information for quick processing.
- They are required for fast execution of arithmetic operations, efficient data handling, and hardware control without frequent access to slower external memory.
- Examples include general-purpose registers (GPRs), stack pointer (SP), and program counter (PC), which play a crucial role in embedded systems and processor operations.

Advanced Microcontroller & Firmware FAQ

11. What is an RTOS, and how does it differ from a bare-metal system?

An RTOS (Real-Time Operating System) manages multiple tasks with precise scheduling, unlike a bare-metal system, which runs a single loop.

Feature	RTOS	Bare-Metal
Multitasking	yes	No
Scheduling	Priority-based	Loop-based
Example	FreeRTOS	Arduino sketches

Example:

FreeRTOS in STM32 allows running sensor tasks, display updates, and communication in parallel.

12. What is Write through cache and write back cache?

Feature	Write-Through Cache	Write-Back Cache
Definition	Data is written simultaneously to both cache and main memory.	Data is first written to the cache and later updated in main memory.
Speed	Slower, as each write goes directly to memory.	Faster, as writes are temporarily stored in cache.
Data Integrity	More reliable, as main memory always has the latest data.	Less reliable if power loss occurs before cache updates memory.
Cache Complexity	Simpler to implement.	More complex, requires tracking dirty bits.

Use Case	Critical applications where data consistency is key (e.g., databases).	Performance-sensitive tasks like gaming, AI, and multimedia processing.

13. How does cache memory improve microcontroller performance?

Cache stores frequently accessed data, reducing memory latency.

Example Usage:

- Instruction Cache (I-Cache) – Speeds up code execution.
- Data Cache (D-Cache) – Reduces RAM access time.

Example:

ARM Cortex-M7 uses L1 cache to improve execution speed.

14. What is a memory leak in firmware, and how do you prevent it?

A memory leak happens when memory is allocated but never released, causing crashes.

Prevention Techniques:

- Avoid dynamic memory allocation (malloc/free) in embedded systems.

- Use static memory allocation for deterministic behavior.

15. What is the difference between SPI and I2C?

Feature	SPI	I2C
Speed	Fasted(10+Mbps)	Slower(400kbps)
Wiring	4 wires(MOSI,MISO,SCLK,CS/SS)	2 wires(SCL,SDA)
Use case	High-speed peripherals(SD cards)	Sensors like temperature, pressure

16. How do you debug firmware using JTAG?

JTAG allows real-time debugging by pausing, inspecting, and modifying registers.

Example:

Developers use Segger J-Link to debug STM32 firmware.

17. What are the key challenges in firmware development?

- Memory constraints – Optimize RAM/Flash usage.
- Real-time execution – Meet strict timing deadlines.
- Power efficiency – Manage low-power modes effectively.

18. What is a CRC check, and why is it used?

Cyclic Redundancy Check (CRC) ensures data integrity in embedded communication.

19. What is firmware over-the-air (FOTA) update, and how does it work?

FOTA allows remote updates of firmware without physical access.

Example:

IoT devices update firmware over Wi-Fi or Bluetooth.

20. What are the best practices for writing efficient embedded firmware?

- Use static memory allocation.
- Minimize ISR execution time.
- Optimize loops and function calls.

Basic RTOS and Real-Time systems FAQ

This section will cover fundamentals of real-time operating systems (RTOS) for beginners and advanced real-time concepts for experienced engineers. Examples are provided wherever necessary for better understanding.

1. What is an RTOS, and how does it differ from a general-purpose OS?

A Real-Time Operating System (RTOS) is designed to process tasks within strict time constraints, ensuring predictable behavior.

Feature	RTOS	General purpose OS
Timing	Deterministic(Real-time)	Non-deterministic
Task Scheduling	Priority based	Time sharing(Fair scheduling)
Example	FreeRTOS, Vxworks	Ubuntu, Windows

Example:

- RTOS in Automotive ECUs: Ensures airbag deployment happens within milliseconds after impact detection.
- General-purpose OS: A video playing on Windows can buffer and is not time-critical.

2. What are the key components of an RTOS?

An RTOS consists of:

1. Task Scheduler – Manages task execution based on priority.
2. Tasks - A small part of the complete program
3. Inter-Task Communication (IPC) – Message queues, semaphores, and mutexes.
4. Timers & Clocks – Used for time-sensitive operations.(software level)
5. Interrupt Service Routines (ISRs) – Handles hardware interrupts.(Hooks provided to handle interrupt in task context instead of interrupt context

Example:

- FreeRTOS task scheduler ensures that a motor control task runs every 10ms, while other background tasks execute when CPU time is available.

- Whenever data received via UART an interrupt will call ISR, in ISR corresponding task will be woken up by releasing semaphore

3. What are the types of real-time systems?

1. Hard Real-Time Systems – Missing a deadline leads to failure (e.g., medical pacemakers, industrial control systems).
2. Soft Real-Time Systems – Missing a deadline reduces performance but doesn't cause failure (e.g., online video streaming).
3. Firm Real-Time Systems – Deadlines are important but missing them occasionally is acceptable (e.g., banking transaction systems).

Example:

- A car's ABS (Anti-lock Braking System) is hard real-time – brakes must activate instantly.
- A video playback app is soft real-time – a slight delay in buffering won't cause failure.

4. How does task scheduling work in an RTOS?

RTOS schedules tasks based on priority rather than fairness.

Common Scheduling Algorithms:

1. Preemptive Scheduling – Highest-priority task runs first (used in RTOS).
2. Round Robin – Tasks get equal time slices (used in general OS).

3. Cooperative Scheduling – Tasks run voluntarily until finished.

Example:

- A temperature control task (high-priority) preempts a data logging task (low-priority) when needed.

5. What are semaphores, and how do they work in RTOS?

A semaphore is a signaling mechanism used for synchronization between tasks.

Type	Function
Binary semaphore	Ensure mutual exclusion
Counting semaphore	Allows multiple tasks to access a resource

Example:

- Binary semaphore is used to control access to a shared SPI bus.
- Counting semaphore manages multiple UART communication buffers.

6. What is a mutex, and how is it different from a semaphore?

A mutex (Mutual Exclusion) is like a binary semaphore, but it ensures that only the task that locks it can unlock it.

Feature	semaphore	Mutex
Ownership	No ownership(any task can unlock)	Task that locks it must unlock it
Priority inversion support	No	Yes
Use case	Task synchronisation	Resource protection

Example:

- A mutex is used to protect shared memory access(critical section) in an RTOS.

7. What is a watchdog timer, and how is it used in RTOS?

A watchdog timer (WDT) resets the system if software crashes or hangs.

Example:

- In an industrial motor controller, if the firmware hangs, the watchdog resets the system to prevent motor damage.

8. What is context switching in an RTOS?

Context switching is the process of saving the current task state and loading another task.

Example:

- In FreeRTOS, when a sensor task is interrupted by a high-priority motor control task, the RTOS saves sensor task data and resumes it later.

9. What is an ISR (Interrupt Service Routine), and how is it used in RTOS?

An ISR is a function that runs immediately when a hardware event occurs.

Example:

- A timer ISR triggers every 1ms to update a real-time clock in an RTOS-based system.

10. What are the advantages of using an RTOS in embedded systems?

- Multitasking support – Multiple tasks run efficiently.
- Real-time scheduling – Critical tasks execute within deadlines.
- Modular development – Easier to debug and scale.

Example:

- A smartwatch uses an RTOS to manage Bluetooth, sensor readings, and display updates efficiently.

Advanced RTOS & Real-Time Systems FAQ

11. What is priority inversion, and how do you solve it in an RTOS?

Priority inversion occurs when a low-priority task holds a resource that a high-priority task needs, delaying execution.

Solution:

- Priority Inheritance – Boosts the low-priority task's priority temporarily.
- Priority Ceiling – Pre-assigns a fixed priority for resource access.

Example:

NASA's Mars Pathfinder mission faced a priority inversion issue, causing unexpected resets.

12. How does an RTOS handle real-time task deadlines?

RTOS uses real-time scheduling policies like Rate Monotonic Scheduling (RMS) and Earliest Deadline First (EDF).

Example:

- Industrial automation systems use RMS to ensure periodic tasks meet deadlines.

13. What is interrupt latency?

Interrupt latency is the time delay between the occurrence of an interrupt and the start of the corresponding Interrupt Service Routine (ISR).

Formula for Interrupt Latency:

Interrupt Latency = Time when ISR starts − Time when interrupt occurs

Interrupt latency is crucial in real-time systems because any delay in handling interrupts can affect system performance, especially in time-sensitive applications like motor control, automotive ECUs, and medical devices.

Example:

Consider a DC motor control system where a sensor generates an interrupt when the motor reaches a certain position.

1. **Interrupt Event:** The sensor detects a position change and triggers an external interrupt (EXTI) to the microcontroller.
2. **Interrupt Latency:** There is a small delay while the CPU finishes executing the current instruction before handling the interrupt.
3. **ISR Execution:** The CPU finally executes the ISR, which adjusts the motor's speed or stops it.

4. If the interrupt latency is too high, the motor may overshoot, leading to inaccurate positioning.

14. What are tickless idle modes in an RTOS?

Tickless mode reduces CPU wake-ups by eliminating periodic RTOS timer interrupts in low-power systems.

Example:

Used in battery-powered IoT sensors to save power.

15. How does an RTOS optimize interrupt latency?

- Disabling nested interrupts
- Using fast ISR execution
- Minimizing context switch overhead

Example:

A robotic arm control system requires low interrupt latency for smooth movement.

16. What is a real-time kernel, and how is it different from a general kernel?

A real-time kernel prioritizes predictable execution over throughput.

Example:

FreeRTOS is an RTOS kernel, while Linux is a general-purpose kernel.

17. What is Inter-Process Communication (IPC) in an RTOS?

IPC allows tasks to communicate via message queues, pipes, and shared memory.

Example:

- A real-time audio processing task sends data to a playback task via a message queue.

18. How do RTOS-based systems handle race conditions?

- Using mutexes for resource protection
- Implementing atomic operations

Example:

Avoiding multiple tasks modifying a shared SPI buffer at the same time.

19. What is the difference between RTOS and bare-metal scheduling?

Feature	RTOS	Bare-Metal
Task switching	Automatic	Manual(Loop-based)
Interrupt Handling	Efficient	Simple but limited

20. What are the key design challenges of RTOS-based systems?

- Timing constraints
- Power efficiency
- Memory optimization

Basic Linux & Embedded Networking FAQ

This section covers fundamental Linux concepts and embedded networking for beginners, followed by advanced topics for experienced engineers. Examples are provided for better understanding.

1. How is embedded Linux different from desktop Linux?

Embedded Linux is a lightweight, optimized version of Linux designed for embedded systems, whereas desktop Linux is built for general computing.

Feature	Embedded Linux	Desktop Linux
Purpose	Used in IoT, industrial devices	Used in PC's, servers
Boot time	Fast(Optimized)	Slow(Has GUI and extra services)
Hardware Support	Specific for SoCs(ARM, MIPS)	General(x86, AMD, ARM)

Example:

- Raspberry Pi runs embedded Linux (Raspbian).
- Ubuntu runs on laptops and desktops.

2. What is the Yocto Project, and why is it used in embedded Linux?

The Yocto Project is a custom Linux distribution builder for embedded systems.

Why Use Yocto?

- Generates small, optimized Linux images.
- Supports cross-compilation for ARM, MIPS, RISC-V.
- Allows customizing kernel, libraries, and filesystem.

Example:

- Automotive infotainment systems use Yocto to build minimal Linux images.

3. What is BusyBox, and why is it used in embedded Linux?

BusyBox is a lightweight replacement for GNU utilities, combining essential Linux commands into a single binary.

Benefits:

- Reduces storage footprint.
- Speeds up system startup.
- Ideal for resource-limited devices.

Example:

- BusyBox is used in embedded routers, IoT devices instead of full Linux utilities.

4. What is a root filesystem in embedded Linux?

The root filesystem (rootfs) contains all necessary system files and libraries for Linux to function.

Example:

- An embedded Linux device loads rootfs from NAND flash or SD card.

5. What is a device tree in Linux, and why is it important?

A device tree (DTB) is a data structure that describes hardware to the Linux kernel.

Why is it needed?

- Allows Linux to boot on different hardware without recompiling the kernel.
- Used in ARM-based embedded systems.

Example:

- A BeagleBone Black board uses a device tree to describe GPIO, I2C, and SPI peripherals.

6. What is U-Boot, and how is it used in embedded Linux?

U-Boot (Universal Bootloader) is a common bootloader for ARM and embedded Linux devices.

Functions:

- Initializes hardware.
- Loads Linux kernel into RAM.
- Supports network booting.

Example:

- U-Boot is used in Raspberry Pi, BeagleBone, and automotive ECUs.

7. What are Linux runlevels, and how are they used in embedded systems?

Runlevels define system states (boot, shutdown, recovery). Some of them are listed below

Run level	Description
0	Halt(shutdown)
1	Single-user mode(Recovery)
3	Multi-user mode (No GUI)
5	Multi-user mode(GUI)

6	Reboot

Example:

- Embedded Linux routers boot into Runlevel 3 (CLI mode).

8. What is cross-compilation, and why is it needed in embedded Linux?

Cross-compilation means compiling software on a different architecture than the target hardware.

Why is it needed?

- Embedded systems (ARM, RISC-V) lack enough processing power to compile software natively.

Example:

- A desktop (x86) compiles code for a Raspberry Pi (ARM) using GCC cross-toolchains.

9. What is TCP/IP, and why is it important in embedded networking?

TCP/IP (Transmission Control Protocol/Internet Protocol) is the foundation of internet communication.

Feature	TCP	UDP

Reliability	yes(Acknowledgement for each packet)	No (Faster)
Use case	Web,emails	Streaming, VoIP

Example:

- Smart home devices use TCP/IP to communicate with cloud servers.

10. What is an embedded web server, and how does it work?

An embedded web server allows a device to serve web-based interfaces.

Example:

- ESP32 microcontrollers host web-based dashboards to monitor sensors.

Advanced Linux & Embedded Networking FAQ

11. How does Linux handle real-time tasks in embedded systems?

Standard Linux is not real-time, but patches like PREEMPT-RT enable low-latency scheduling.

Example:

- A robotic control system uses PREEMPT-RT for precise motor timing.

12. What is the difference between static and dynamic linking in embedded systems?

Type	Static Linking	Dynamic Linking
size	Larger binary	Smaller binary
performance	Faster startup	Slower(Needs library loading)

Example:

- Embedded firmware uses static linking for standalone execution.

13. What is network socket programming in embedded systems?

Sockets enable network communication between devices.

Example:

- A Raspberry Pi server communicates with an ESP32 IoT device via sockets(TCP/UDP).

14. What is CAN bus and its importance in embedded networking?

CAN (Controller Area Network) is a real-time communication protocol used in automotive and industrial systems.

Example:

- Modern cars use CAN to transfer engine sensor data between ECUs.

15. What is IPv6, and why is it used in embedded networking?

IPv6 replaces IPv4 to support more devices and improve security.

Example:

- IoT devices use IPv6 to connect to smart home networks.

16. What is MQTT, and how does it work in embedded IoT systems?

MQTT (Message Queuing Telemetry Transport) is a lightweight protocol for IoT communication.

Example:

- Smart home sensors use MQTT to send data to cloud dashboards.

17. What is a real-time Ethernet protocol, and where is it used?

Real-time Ethernet (PROFINET, EtherCAT) is used in industrial automation to meet time-sensitive communication requirements.

Example:

- Robotic arms in manufacturing plants use EtherCAT for real-time control.

18. How do embedded systems handle network security?

Embedded devices use:

- TLS encryption (for secure HTTPS).
- Firewall rules (to block unauthorized access).
- Over-the-air (OTA) updates (to fix security vulnerabilities).

Example:

- A smart thermostat encrypts MQTT messages to prevent hacking.

19. What is NAT, and how does it help embedded networked devices?

Network Address Translation (NAT) allows multiple devices to share a single public IP.

Example:

- Home routers use NAT to connect multiple IoT devices to the internet.

20. What are the biggest challenges in embedded Linux and networking?

- Limited resources (low RAM, CPU power).
- Security vulnerabilities in connected devices.
- Real-time constraints in networked embedded systems.

Example:

- Medical devices must ensure real-time data transmission with strict security.

Basic Debugging & Optimization FAQ

This section covers fundamentals of debugging and optimization techniques for beginners, followed by advanced debugging strategies for experienced engineers. Examples are provided for better understanding.

1. What are the common debugging techniques in embedded systems?

Debugging in embedded systems involves analyzing and fixing issues at the hardware and firmware level.

Common Debugging Methods:

1. Print Debugging (UART, Serial Logs) – Using printf() or Serial.print() to track execution.
2. LED Debugging – Flashing LEDs at key points to indicate system state.
3. Breakpoints & Step Debugging – Using a debugger to pause and inspect execution.
4. Oscilloscope & Logic Analyzers – Capturing signals for timing issues.
5. JTAG/SWD Debugging – Using hardware debuggers to inspect memory and registers.

Example:

- Using UART logs to debug firmware crashes in an STM32-based system.

2. What is JTAG, and how is it used in debugging?

JTAG (Joint Test Action Group) is a hardware debugging protocol that allows real-time inspection of a running embedded system.

How JTAG Helps Debugging:

- Step through code execution line-by-line.
- Read and write memory & registers in real time.
- Debug without modifying firmware code.

Example:

- Using Segger J-Link with JTAG to debug an ARM Cortex-M firmware issue.

3. What is a logic analyzer, and when should it be used?

A logic analyzer is a tool that captures digital signals to analyze communication protocols like UART, SPI, and I2C.

Use Cases:

- Debugging communication errors between microcontroller and peripherals.
- Checking timing violations in real-time applications.

Example:

- Using a Saleae Logic Analyzer to debug SPI communication errors in an IoT sensor.

4. What is a watchdog timer, and how does it help debugging?

A watchdog timer (WDT) resets the system if the firmware crashes or gets stuck in an infinite loop.

Example:

- In an industrial automation system, the watchdog resets the system if a sensor task stops responding.

5. How can you detect and fix stack overflows in embedded systems?

A stack overflow occurs when a function call depth exceeds allocated stack memory, causing system crashes.

Prevention Techniques:

- Use stack size monitoring (RTOS provides stack usage stats).
- Avoid deep recursion and use iterative algorithms instead.
- Enable stack overflow detection in development tools.

Example:

- An RTOS task runs out of stack while processing large JSON data, causing a system reset.

6. What is memory leakage, and how can you avoid it?

A memory leak happens when allocated memory is not freed, leading to system slowdowns or crashes.

Prevention Techniques:

- Use static memory allocation instead of malloc/free in embedded systems.
- Track memory usage using heap analyzers.

Example:

- An IoT device leaks memory after every API call, eventually crashing after a few days.

7. What are the common causes of embedded system crashes?

- Null pointer dereference (accessing invalid memory).
- Stack overflows (deep recursion).
- Race conditions (improper shared resource access).
- Hardware failures (bad power supply, overheating).

Example:

- A buggy ISR corrupts memory, causing a random system crash.

8. How do you optimize power consumption in embedded systems?

- Use low-power sleep modes.
- Disable unused peripherals.

- Use dynamic frequency scaling.

Example:

- A battery-powered sensor node enters deep sleep mode between data transmissions.

9. What are the best practices for optimizing embedded firmware?

- Use efficient data structures.
- Avoid floating-point operations (use fixed-point math instead).
- Optimize loops and function calls.

Example:

- Rewriting a slow floating-point math function in fixed-point increased speed by 30%.

10. What are the common compiler optimization techniques in embedded systems?

- Loop unrolling (reduces loop overhead).
- Function inlining (reduces function call overhead).
- Dead code elimination (removes unused code).

Example:

- GCC compiler's -O2 flag optimizes embedded firmware for speed and size.

Advanced Debugging & Optimization FAQ

11. What is real-time tracing, and how is it used in debugging?

Real-time tracing captures system execution without stopping it, helping debug real-time applications.

Example:

- Using STM32 RTOS view to trace FreeRTOS task execution.

12. What is a race condition, and how do you debug it?

A race condition occurs when multiple tasks access shared resources incorrectly, leading to unpredictable behavior.

Fixes:

- Use mutexes/semaphores for resource protection.
- Use volatile keyword for variables which can be changed by external entity.

Example:

- Two RTOS tasks updating a global counter at the same time cause incorrect results.

13. What are atomic operations, and why are they important?

Atomic operations ensure single-instruction execution without interruption, preventing race conditions.

Example:

- Using __atomic_add() in ARM Cortex-M to safely increment a shared variable.

14. How do you debug interrupts in embedded systems?

- Use GPIO toggling to measure ISR execution time.
- Enable ISR logging using hardware trace analyzers.

Example:

- A high-priority ISR is delaying low-priority tasks, leading to system lag.

15. How do you analyze memory fragmentation in embedded systems?

Memory fragmentation wastes RAM, reducing system stability.

Fixes:

- Use fixed-size memory pools.
- Minimize dynamic allocations.

Example:

- A system crashes after a few days due to heap fragmentation from frequent malloc/free calls.

16. What is function inlining, and when should it be used?

Function inlining replaces function calls with actual code, reducing overhead.

Example:

- A small delay function is inlined to avoid function call overhead in a real-time system.

17. How do you analyze CPU load in an embedded system?

- Use profiling tools like FreeRTOS Tracealyzer.
- Monitor task execution time using system timers.

Example:

- An overutilized CPU causes missed deadlines in a real-time motor control system.

18. How do you optimize ISR execution time?

- Keep ISRs short and fast.
- Offload complex processing to background tasks.

Example:

- Moving UART data processing from ISR to a task improved system responsiveness.

19. What are the challenges of debugging low-power embedded systems?

- Debugging tools consume power, affecting real-world behavior.
- Sleep modes disable debugging interfaces (JTAG, UART).

Example:

- An IoT sensor works in lab tests but fails in the field due to different power conditions.

20. What are the key performance bottlenecks in embedded firmware, and how do you resolve them?

Bottleneck	Solution
Slow memory access	Use DMA, optimize cache usage
Expensive floating point operations	Use fixed-point arithmetic
Inefficient loops	Optimize loop conditions

Example:

- A machine vision system optimized memory access by using DMA, improving processing speed.

Advice for embedded system aspirants

This section covers fundamental interview preparation tips for beginners and advanced career strategies for experienced engineers.

1. What are the most common mistakes candidates make in embedded systems interviews?

- Lack of hands-on experience – Focusing only on theory.
- Not preparing for debugging scenarios – Real-world embedded work is debugging-heavy.
- Ignoring memory constraints – Writing inefficient code for microcontrollers with limited RAM/Flash.

Example:

- A candidate writes a recursive function on an 8-bit microcontroller, leading to a stack overflow.

2. How should I prepare for an embedded systems interview?

1. Understand microcontroller architecture (Registers, GPIOs, Timers, Interrupts).
2. Practice C programming for embedded (bitwise operations, memory management).
3. Study RTOS concepts (tasks, scheduling, mutexes).
4. Work on real projects (Build firmware for an IoT sensor).

Example:

- Write an embedded C program to control an LED with a push button using interrupts.

3. What are the key topics I should study before an embedded interview?

Category	Topics
C programming	Pointers, structs, bitwise operations
Microcontrollers	GPIO, Timers, Interrupts, Flash/RAM
RTOS	Scheduling, Mutexes, semaphores
Communication	UART,SPI,I2C,CAN
Debugging	JTAG, Logic analyzers, WDT

4. What kind of projects can help me get an embedded job?

- Build a sensor-based IoT device (ESP32 + Temperature sensor + Cloud).
- Write an RTOS-based application (Task scheduling, message queues).

- Create a simple motor control system (PWM control).

5. How should I explain my embedded project in an interview?

Follow the STAR method:

1. Situation – What problem did you solve?
2. Task – What was your role?
3. Action – What approach did you take?
4. Result – What was the outcome?

Example:

- I designed an energy-efficient IoT sensor that entered deep sleep mode, reducing power consumption by 60%.

6. How do I answer behavioral questions in an embedded interview?

Employers assess problem-solving skills and teamwork.

Common Questions:

- Tell me about a time you debugged a difficult issue.
- How do you handle tight deadlines in embedded development?

Example Answer:

- I once debugged a random firmware crash by using JTAG to inspect register values, leading to the discovery of a null pointer dereference.

7. What are the key skills embedded companies look for in freshers?

- C Programming
- Hands-on experience with microcontrollers (ARM, STM32, ESP32)
- Basic RTOS concepts
- Understanding of communication protocols (UART, I2C, SPI)

8. Should I learn assembly language for embedded jobs?

- For basic firmware development, assembly is not mandatory.
- For low-level optimization (bootloaders, DSP), knowledge of ARM/AVR assembly is useful.

9. How do I showcase my embedded skills on my resume?

- Mention hands-on projects – Built a wireless sensor node using STM32 and LoRaWAN.
- Highlight debugging experience – Used JTAG to debug firmware issues in an automotive ECU.
- Include relevant tools – Experience with FreeRTOS, Keil, GCC, and CAN bus analysis.

Example:

- Developed an embedded RTOS-based application to monitor machine vibrations in an industrial setup.

10. How do I transition from firmware development to embedded security?

1. Learn secure boot and firmware encryption.
2. Understand hardware security modules (HSMs).
3. Study IoT device security and secure OTA updates.

11. What is the best way to advance from an embedded developer to an embedded architect?

- Gain deep expertise in firmware, RTOS, and low-level drivers.
- Learn system design principles (bootloaders, BSP, kernel internals).
- Mentor junior engineers.

12. Should I learn Linux kernel development for embedded career growth?

- If working with embedded Linux (Raspberry Pi, BeagleBone), YES.
- For bare-metal microcontroller development, it's optional.

13. What certifications help in an embedded systems career?

- ARM Accredited Engineer (AAE) – For ARM Cortex development.
- Embedded Linux Foundation Certification – For Linux-based embedded careers.
- Certified IoT Professional (CIoTP) – IoT-specific.

14. How do I negotiate a better salary in embedded systems jobs?

- Highlight expertise in low-level optimizations, debugging, and RTOS.
- Showcase real-world contributions (e.g., "Optimized power consumption by 40% in IoT firmware").
- Leverage offers from multiple companies.

15. How important is FPGA knowledge for embedded engineers?

- Useful for high-speed applications (DSP, AI accelerators, networking).
- Less relevant for general firmware engineering.

16. How can I contribute to open-source embedded projects?

- Contribute to RTOS projects (Zephyr, FreeRTOS).
- Help with Linux kernel device drivers.
- Publish firmware libraries on GitHub.

17. What is the future of embedded systems?

- AI + Embedded (Edge AI, TinyML)
- 5G & IoT connectivity

- Cybersecurity in embedded devices
- Space tech's and aviations

18. How can I transition into automotive embedded systems?

- Learn AUTOSAR, CAN bus, functional safety (ISO 26262).
- Work on ECU firmware and automotive diagnostics (UDS protocol).

Example:

- Develop an automotive headlight control system using CAN bus.

19. What are the key differences between startup and enterprise embedded roles?

Feature	Startup	Enterprise
Project Scope	Broad(Hardware + software)	Narrow(Either Software or Hardware, even a single part in complete firmware)
Workload	High	Managed
Learning	Fast-paced	Structured

Basic Embedded Systems Projects For Beginners

1. LED Blinking with a Microcontroller

- Objective: Blink an LED at different intervals using an Arduino or STM32.
- Components: Microcontroller board, LED, resistor, jumper wires.
- Expected Outcome: Understanding of GPIO control and delays.

2. Push Button Controlled LED

- Objective: Use a push button to toggle an LED on/off.
- Components: Microcontroller, push button, LED, resistor.
- Expected Outcome: Learn digital input handling and debouncing techniques.

3. PWM-Based LED Dimming

- Objective: Control LED brightness using Pulse Width Modulation (PWM).
- Components: Microcontroller, LED, resistor.
- Expected Outcome: Understanding of PWM and duty cycles.

4. Temperature Sensor with Display

- Objective: Read temperature using a DHT11/LM35 sensor and display it on an LCD.

- Components: DHT11/LM35, LCD/OLED, microcontroller.
- Expected Outcome: Learn sensor interfacing and data display techniques.

5. Serial Communication (UART with PC)

- Objective: Send and receive data via UART using an embedded system.
- Components: Microcontroller, USB-to-Serial adapter.
- Expected Outcome: Understanding of serial communication protocols.

6. 7-Segment Display Counter

- Objective: Display numbers incrementing every second on a 7-segment display.
- Components: 7-segment display, microcontroller.
- Expected Outcome: Learn multiplexing and digital output control.

7. Buzzer Alarm System

- Objective: Use a buzzer to generate an alarm when a button is pressed.
- Components: Buzzer, button, microcontroller.
- Expected Outcome: Understanding of digital outputs and sound alerts.

8. IR Sensor-Based Object Detection

- Objective: Detect objects using an IR proximity sensor.
- Components: IR sensor, microcontroller.
- Expected Outcome: Learn sensor interfacing and object detection techniques.

9. Capacitive Touch Sensor Interface

- Objective: Interface a capacitive touch sensor to trigger an LED/buzzer.
- Components: Capacitive touch sensor, microcontroller.
- Expected Outcome: Learn touch input handling and digital interfacing.

10. Analog to Digital Conversion (ADC) with Potentiometer

- Objective: Convert analog input from a potentiometer into digital values.
- Components: Potentiometer, microcontroller.
- Expected Outcome: Learn ADC functionality in microcontrollers.

Advanced Embedded Systems Projects

1. IoT-Based Weather Station

- Objective: Collect temperature, humidity, and pressure data and send it to the cloud.
- Components: ESP32, DHT11, BMP280, MQTT server.
- Expected Outcome: Understanding of IoT protocols and cloud data integration.

2. RTOS-Based Task Scheduler

- Objective: Implement FreeRTOS to manage multiple tasks (e.g., LED blinking + UART communication).
- Components: Microcontroller, FreeRTOS.
- Expected Outcome: Learn real-time scheduling and multitasking.

3. CAN Bus Communication Between Two MCUs

- Objective: Interface two STM32/PIC microcontrollers via CAN bus.
- Components: Two MCUs with CAN support, transceivers.
- Expected Outcome: Understanding of CAN protocol and inter-device communication.

4. Voice-Controlled Home Automation

- Objective: Use ESP32 with Alexa/Google Assistant to control appliances.
- Components: ESP32, relay module, smart assistant.
- Expected Outcome: Learn voice command integration with embedded systems.

5. Gesture-Based Control Using IMU (MPU6050)

- Objective: Control a robot or cursor using hand gestures.
- Components: IMU sensor, microcontroller.
- Expected Outcome: Learn motion sensing and gesture recognition.

6. Low-Power Battery Optimization for IoT Devices

- Objective: Implement deep sleep mode to optimize battery life.
- Components: Low-power MCU (ESP32, STM32L), battery.
- Expected Outcome: Learn power management techniques.

7. SD Card Data Logging System

- Objective: Store sensor readings on an SD card with time stamps.
- Components: Microcontroller, SD card module, RTC.
- Expected Outcome: Learn file handling and real-time data logging.

8. AI on Edge (TinyML with Microcontrollers)

- Objective: Implement image classification or anomaly detection on an MCU.
- Components: ESP32/STM32 with TinyML, camera/sensors.
- Expected Outcome: Learn machine learning on embedded devices.

9. Automated Water Level Monitoring & Control System

- Objective: Use ultrasonic sensors + pumps to automate water tanks.
- Components: Ultrasonic sensor, relay module, microcontroller.
- Expected Outcome: Learn sensor-based automation and control systems.

10. Drone Stabilization Using PID Controller

- Objective: Implement PID control for flight stability using an IMU sensor.
- Components: Flight controller, IMU sensor.
- Expected Outcome: Learn PID tuning for precise control systems.

Conclusion & Final Thoughts

This section wraps up the book, reinforcing key takeaways and providing next steps for readers to continue growing in embedded systems.

1. Summary of Key Learnings

Throughout this book, we have covered 100 essential FAQs across various embedded systems topics, including:

- Embedded Basics – Microcontrollers, memory, and interrupts.
- Firmware Development – RTOS, device drivers, and power optimization.
- Embedded Linux & Networking – Kernel internals, TCP/IP, and IoT protocols.
- Debugging & Optimization – JTAG, logic analyzers, and performance tuning.
- Interview & Career Advice – How to prepare, negotiate salaries, and advance in your career.

Each section provided real-world examples to help bridge the gap between theory and practical implementation.

2. What's Next? Continuing Your Embedded Systems Journey

To truly master embedded systems, continuous learning and hands-on experience are required. Here's how you can keep improving:

A. Work on Real-World Projects

B. Deep Dive into Specific Topics

Based on your career goals, focus on advanced areas like:

Career path	Skills to Focus On
Embedded Firmware Engineer	RTOS, MCU programming, power optimization
Embedded Linux Developer	Kernel programming, device drivers, yocto
Automotive Embedded Engineer	AUTOSAR, CAN, Functional safety (ISO 26262)
IoT & wireless system engineer	Low-power wireless protocols like BLE,LoRa, Zigbee
AI on embedded systems	Edge AI, TinyML, TensorFlow Lite

C. Contribute to Open-Source Projects

Become an active contributor in embedded communities.

- Submit bug fixes or improvements to FreeRTOS, Zephyr, or Linux Kernel.
- Publish firmware libraries on GitHub (e.g., UART drivers, sensor libraries).
- Write technical blogs or create video tutorials on embedded topics.

3. Final Words of Advice

Embedded systems engineering is a journey, not a destination.

- Stay curious – New technologies like AI on microcontrollers and 5G IoT are emerging.
- Build, break, and debug – Experience is the best teacher.
- Network with experts – Join forums like Stack Overflow, IEEE groups, and LinkedIn communities.

4. A Note to the Reader

If you found this book helpful, consider leaving a review on Amazon. Your feedback helps improve future editions and assists other engineers in learning embedded systems.

If you have questions, corrections, or suggestions, feel free to:

■ Email: faayizm98@gmail.com

Thank you for reading, and best of luck in your embedded systems journey!